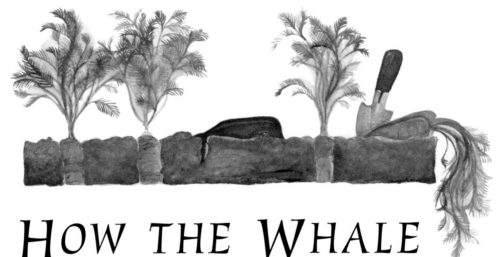

HOW THE WHALE BECAME

BECAME

and Other Stories

TED HUGHES

HOW THE WHALE BECAME
and Other Stories

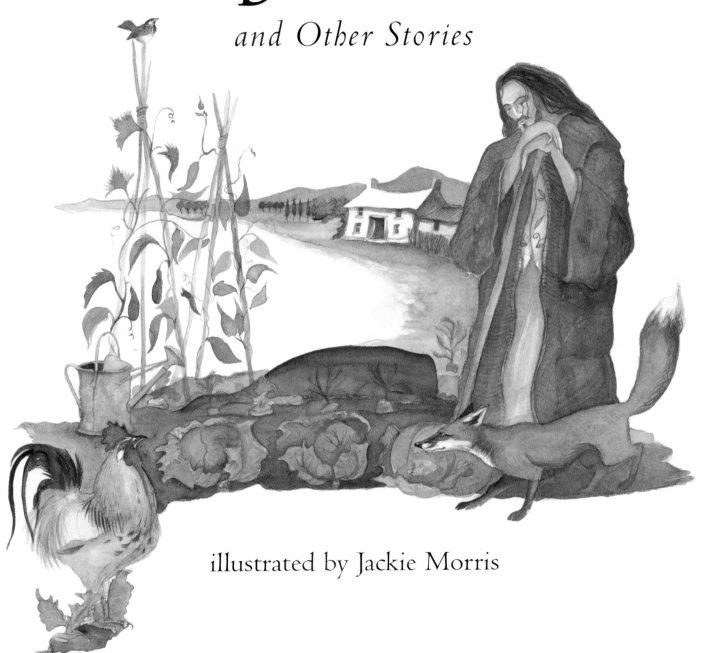

illustrated by Jackie Morris

ff

For Thomas and Hannah

J.M.

First published in 1963
This illustrated edition first published in 2000
by Faber and Faber Limited
3 Queen Square, London, WC1N 3AU

Origination: Miles Kelly Publishing
Designer: Sarah Hodder
Colour Reproduction: DPI Colour

A CIP record for this book
is available from the British Library

ISBN 0-571-20200-4

2 4 6 8 10 9 7 5 3 1

For Frieda and Nicholas

A NOTE FROM THE PUBLISHER

Ted Hughes started writing these creation fables in 1956
when he and his first wife Sylvia Plath were in Spain
shortly after their marriage, though the stories in this book
were not published until 1963 after the birth
of their two children, Frieda and Nicholas.

The themes in these fables are ones that the author returned to
again and again in his writing for the young: pride, envy, greed,
and how to overcome such shortcomings; how to be comfortable
with yourself, and to make the best of one's own abilities.

Ted Hughes was a champion of children — his commitment to their
development and self-awareness is well-known.
He always found time to encourage, and never patronised.
The pleasure he derived from writing for children
and reading to children resonates from these pages.

CONTENTS

CONTENTS

Long ago when the world was brand new, before animals or birds, the sun rose into the sky and brought the first day.

The flowers jumped up and stared round astonished. Then from every side, from under leaves and from behind rocks, creatures began to appear.

In those days the colours were much better than they are now, much brighter. And the air sparkled because it had never been used.

But don't think everything was so easy.

To begin with, all the creatures were pretty much alike — very different from what they are now. They had no idea what they were going to become. Some wanted to become linnets, some wanted to become lions, some wanted to become other things. The ones that wanted to become lions practised at being lions — and by and by, sure enough, they began to turn into lions. So, the ones that wanted to become linnets practised at being linnets, and slowly they turned into linnets. And so on.

But there were other creatures that came about in other ways ...

WHY THE OWL
BEHAVES
AS IT DOES

WHEN OWL BECAME AN OWL, the first thing he discovered was that he could see by night. The next thing he discovered was that none of the other birds could.

They could see only by day. They knew it was no use trying to see by dark night, so at every grey dusk they closed their eyes and slept until the grey dawn. They had been doing this for so long, they had forgotten what the dark was.

Owl thought about this. Then he went to the other birds and said: 'I know a country where there are farms, but no farmers. You may eat when and where you please. There are no guns, no bird-scarers, no men. I will take you there if you like.'

Every day, Man killed large numbers of the birds as they were feeding in the fields. They said:

'This sounds like a safe, peaceful country, made for birds. Let us go with Owl.'

Owl smiled to himself.

'Good,' he said. 'Now, as we have no passports, we shall have to cross the frontier by night, when no one can see us. We shall leave at dusk and should be there by dawn.'

When dusk came, Owl led all the birds to a rabbit hole on the hill.

'Hold each other's hands,' he cried. 'I will lead you.'

All the rabbits that lived on the hill ran up to see what new game the birds were playing. Owl led the way down into the dark hole.

'Is this night, then?' whispered the linnets in the pitchy darkness of the hole.

'Hmm,' said the crows. 'So this is night.'

It was so dark down the hole that the birds couldn't even see their own beaks. Each one clung to the wing of the bird in front and followed blindly. Owl led them to and fro in the loops and twists of the hole for about five minutes. By that time, the birds, who were not at all used to walking, felt as if they had been travelling for hours.

'Is it much further?' cried the swallows. 'Oh, our poor little feet!'

At last Owl shouted:

'Halt, while I see if it's all clear up ahead.'

He popped his head out of the rabbit hole and looked around. It was darker than when they had entered the hole a few minutes before, but it was not yet quite night. There was still a pale light in the west.

'Here we are!' he cried then. 'Over the border, just as dawn is breaking.'

And he led the birds out into the open. All the rabbits ran up again and sat, one ear up and one ear down, watching the birds with very puzzled expressions.

'Is this the new country?' asked the birds, and they crept close together, looking round at the almost dark landscape.

'This is it,' said Owl. 'And that is dawn you can see breaking in the East.'

The birds had quite lost their bearings in the dark underground, and the landscape was now too dark to recognize as the one they knew so well by day. They believed everything that Owl said.

Owl led them off the hill and down towards a farm.

'But it seems to be getting darker,' said the doves suddenly.

'Ah, I am glad you noticed that,' said Owl. 'That is something I forgot to tell you. In this country, day is darker than dawn.'

He smiled to himself, but the birds looked at each other in dismay.

'But what about the nights?' they cried. 'If day is darker than dawn, how dark are the nights?'

Owl stopped and looked at them. They couldn't see his face, but they could tell he was very serious.

'Night here,' he said, 'is so dark, so terribly dark, that it is impossible for a mere bird to survive one glimpse of it. There is only one thing to do if you want to keep alive. You must close your eyes as tight as you can as soon as the dark of the day begins to turn grey. You must keep them closed until I awake you at grey dawn. One peep at the dark, and you are dead birds.'

Then, without another word, he led them into the stackyard of the farm.

The farm lights were out. The farmer was sleeping. The farm was silent.

'Here you are,' said Owl. 'Just as I promised. Now feed.'

The birds scratched and pecked, but by now it was too dark to see a thing. At last they learned to find the grains by feeling with their feet. But it was slow work.

Meanwhile Owl sat on the corner of the barn, overlooking the stackyard. Whenever he felt like it, he dropped down and snatched up a nightingale or a willow-warbler. In the pitch dark, the rest of the birds were no wiser. 'This is better than rats and mice and beetles,' said Owl, as he cleaned the blood from his beak. By the time the first grey light showed in the sky, Owl was fuller than he had ever been in his life.

He gave a shout:

'Here comes the grey of dusk. Hurry, hurry! We must get to our beds and close our eyes before the terrible dark comes.'

Tumbling over each other and bumping into things, the birds ran towards his voice. When they were all gathered, he led them to a near-by copse which was full of brambles.

'Here is good roosting,' said Owl. 'I will awaken you at dawn.'

And so, in the grey of dawn, which Owl had told them was the grey of dusk, the birds closed their eyes. All that bright day they stood in groups under the brambles, their eyes tightly closed. Some of them were too frightened to fall asleep. Not one of them dared to open an eye. One look at that darkness, Owl had said, and you are dead birds.

Owl dozed happily in the dark hollow of a tree. His trick was working perfectly. He was very pleased with himself. No more mice and rats and beetles for him.

At dusk he gave a shout.

'Here is dawn,' he told the birds. 'Back to our feeding.'

And he led them back to the farm where everything happened as the night before.

In this way, Owl grew fat and contented, while the other birds grew wretched.

They grew tired of scraping in the dark stackyard. Sometimes they swallowed a grain, but as often it was a cinder. The farm cocks and hens that picked the stackyard over from end to end all day long had not left much for the birds.

And when they fell asleep, they were terrified lest they have a dream, open their eyes without thinking, and catch a glimpse of the deadly darkness. It was a great strain. Owl was continually warning them of the danger.

'One peep at that darkness,' he kept saying, 'and you are dead birds.'

If only one little bird had peeped, for only one second, with only one eye, he would have seen that there was no such thing as deadly darkness. He would have seen the sun, and the countryside he knew so well. But Owl made sure that none ever did.

The birds grew thin. Their feathers began to fall out. Their feet ached with stumbling about in the darkness, and their wings ached with never being used. They did not like the new country.

They complained among themselves.

At last, one dusk, when Owl awoke them with his usual cry: 'Dawn!' they all went up to him and told him they could stand it no longer.

'Please lead us back to our own country,' said the birds.

Owl was worried. He wanted to keep the birds in his power. He didn't want to go back to eating rats, mice and beetles.

Then he had an idea.

'Yes,' he said. 'You are right. This is a fine country, and not dangerous. But, as you say, it is hard to make a living here. Let us find the hole by which we came and return to our own country.'

He led them up to the rabbit warren on the hill. It was almost dark.

'Here are the birds playing that game again,' said the rabbits, and they all ran up to stare.

'Now,' said Owl to the birds. 'It was one of these holes, but just which one I cannot remember. Can any of you remember?'

'I think it might have been this one,' said Cuckoo.

'Or perhaps this one,' said Jenny Wren.

'Let us try them all,' said Owl.

Most of the birds didn't dare to enter the holes lest they get lost. The ones that did were soon up again saying:

'This one comes out here.'

And:

'This one comes out here.'

Owl pretended to be distressed.

'We have lost our way back, and it is all my fault. Oh dear!' he cried. Then he made his voice sound very brave, as he said:

'As we are here for good, let us make the best of it.'

And he led them down to the stackyard for the night's feeding.

So it went on, for almost a year.

At last the birds decided they had had enough. They were too unhappy to go on living.

'This is no life whatsoever,' they said to each other.

'Let us all die bravely, and at once,' said Robin, 'rather than go on dying slowly in this miserable way.'

'We will do that!' cried the storm-cocks. 'Let us all die bravely together, rather than live like this.'

'But how?' said little Gold-Crested Wren. 'How can we die?'

'Let us open our eyes,' said Robin, 'to the deadly darkness. Owl said that will kill us all.'

The unhappy birds went out with Owl that night for the last time. He led them to the stackyard as usual, and took up his post. But instead of trying to find food, the birds all sat down together in a big close group in the middle of the yard. They had decided what to do. But Owl knew nothing of it. He stared down. Softly, the birds began to sing their old songs.

'What's the matter with you?' cried Owl. 'You'll starve if you don't eat!'

But the birds took no notice of him. They went on singing, in their thin, hungry voices. It was a long time since they had sung. Now they sang very low, and very sadly.

It was a bright night, with a full moon, but Owl couldn't catch a single one of those birds. They were pressed far too closely one against another. He couldn't even pick one from the edge of the group. And they sang all night long.

By dawn Owl was furious.

'Dusk!' he cried. 'Back to the copse! Here comes the deadly dark.'

He was very hungry. But he knew what he would do. He would sneak down on them by broad day, when they were standing under the brambles with their eyes tight shut. Then he would eat his fill. He would have a song-thrush, a yellow-hammer, a greenfinch, and five bluetits —

'Where are you going?' he cried.

Instead of following him back to the copse, the birds had turned up the hill. Following the rising ground, they came at last to the very top. All around them lay the dark landscape. They gathered under the three elm trees there and faced the first grey line that was showing in the East. Then, once more, they began to sing their old songs.

Soon the deadly darkness would begin to spread through the sky. Or so they thought. They stared into the brightening dawn and sang, holding their eyes as wide as they could to catch the first rays of deadly darkness.

Oh, they were so tired of their lives.

To die like this was better than to live as they had been doing, going nowhere but where Owl led them, always in darkness, scraping their feet raw for a few grains.

They sang, and stared into the dawn. Every moment they expected the first killing ray of black to shoot out of the bright East.

At the edge of the field Owl was beating his head with his wings. He knew what the result would be. In a few minutes the sun would rise, and the birds would recognize the landscape round them.

'Come home!' he cried. 'You sillies! You'll all be killed dead as stones. Come home and close your eyes!'

But the birds had no more interest in anything that Owl said. They only wanted to die.

Slowly the sun put its burning red edge into the sky.

Lark gave a shriek. He sprang up into the air.

'It's the sun!' he cried. 'It's real day!'

Slowly the sun rose.

As it rose, the birds flew up into the branches of the elms, dancing on the twigs, and singing till their heads rang.

'It's the sun!' they sang. 'It's real day!'

From under a blackthorn bush at the field's edge, Owl stared in rage. Then he ducked his head, and flew away from the hedge, low over the ground. Even so, the birds saw him.

'He tricked us!' they cried. 'And there he goes! There goes the trickster!'

In a shouting mob, all the birds flocked after Owl. All the way back to his tree they beat him with their wings, and pulled out his feathers. He buried himself deep in his hollow tree.

The birds flew up into the tree top and sang on.

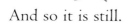

And so it is still.

Every morning the birds sing, and the Owl flies back to his dark hole. When the birds see him, they mob him, remembering his trick. He dare come out only at night, to scrape a bare living on rats, mice and beetles.

HOW the WHALE
BECAME

Now God had a little back-garden. In this garden he grew
carrots, onions, beans and whatever else he needed for his dinner.
It was a fine little garden. The plants were in neat rows, and a tidy
fence kept out the animals. God was pleased with it.

One day as he was weeding the carrots he saw a strange thing between the
rows. It was no more than an inch long, and it was black. It was like a black
shiny bean. At one end it had a little root going into the ground.

'That's very odd,' said God. 'I've never seen one of these before. I wonder
what it will grow into.'

So he left it growing.

Next day, as he was gardening, he remembered the little shiny black thing.
He went to see how it was getting on. He was surprised. During the night it
had doubled its length. It was two inches long, like a shiny black egg.

Every day God went to look at it, and every day it was bigger. Every
morning, in fact, it was just twice as long as it had been the morning before.

When it was six feet long, God said:

'It's getting too big. I must pull it up and cook it.'

But he left it a day.

Next day it was twelve feet long and far too big to go into any of God's pans.

God stood scratching his head and looking at it. Already it had crushed
most of his carrots out of sight. If it went on growing at this rate it would
soon be pushing his house over.

Suddenly, as he looked at it, it opened an eye and looked at him.

God was amazed.

The eye was quite small and round. It was near the thickest end, and farthest
from the root. He walked round to the other side, and there was another eye,
also looking at him.

'Well!' said God. 'And how do you do?'

The round eye blinked, and the smooth glossy skin under it
wrinkled slightly, as if the thing were smiling. But there was no
mouth, so God wasn't sure.

Next morning God rose early and went out into his garden.

Sure enough, during the night his new black plant with eyes had doubled its length again. It had pushed down part of his fence, so that its head was sticking out into the road, one eye looking up it, and one down. Its side was pressed against the kitchen wall.

God walked round to its front and looked it in the eye.

'You are too big,' he said sternly. 'Please stop growing before you push my house down.'

To his surprise the plant opened a mouth. A long slit of a mouth, which ran back on either side under the eyes.

'I can't,' said the mouth.

God didn't know what to say. At last he said:

'Well then, can you tell me what sort of a thing you are? Do you know?'

'I,' said the thing, 'am Whale-Wort. You have heard of Egg-Plant, and Buck-Wheat, and Dog-Daisy. Well, I am Whale-Wort.'

There was nothing God could do about that.

By next morning, Whale-Wort stretched right across the road, and his side had pushed the kitchen wall into the kitchen. He was now longer and fatter than a bus.

When God saw this, he called the creatures together.

'Here's a strange thing,' he said. 'Look at it. What are we going to do with it?'

The creatures walked round Whale-Wort, looking at him. His skin was so shiny they could see their faces in it.

'Leave it,' suggested Ostrich. 'And wait till it dies down.'

'But it might go on growing,' said God. 'Until it covers the whole earth. We shall have to live on its back. Think of that.'

'I suggest,' said Mouse, 'that we throw it into the sea.'

God thought.

'No,' he said at last. 'That's too severe. Let's just leave it for a few days.'

After three more days, God's house was completely flat, and Whale-Wort was as long as a street.

'Now,' said Mouse, 'it is too late to throw it into the sea. Whale-Wort is too big to move.'

But God fastened long thick ropes round him and called up all the creatures to help haul on the ends.

'Hey!' cried Whale-Wort. 'Leave me alone.'

'You are going into the sea,' cried Mouse. 'And it serves you right. Taking up all this space.'

'But I'm happy!' cried Whale-Wort again. 'I'm happy just lying here. Leave me and let me sleep. I was made just to lie and sleep.'

'Into the sea!' cried Mouse.

'No!' cried Whale-Wort.

'Into the sea!' cried all the creatures. And they hauled on the ropes. With a great groan, Whale-Wort's root came out of the ground. He began to thresh and twist, beating down houses and trees with his long root, as the creatures dragged him willy-nilly through the countryside.

At last they got him to the top of a high cliff. With a great shout they rolled him over the edge and into the sea.

'Help! Help!' cried Whale-Wort. 'I shall drown! Please let me come back on land where I can sleep.'

'Not until you're smaller!' shouted God. 'Then you can come back.'

'But how am I to get smaller?' wept Whale-Wort, as he rolled to and fro in the sea. 'Please show me how to get smaller so that I can live on land.'

God bent down from the high cliff and poked Whale-Wort on the top of his head with his finger.

'Ow!' cried Whale-Wort. 'What was that for? You've made a hole. The water will come in.'

'No it won't, said God. 'But some of you will come out. Now just you start blowing some of yourself out through that hole.'

Whale-Wort blew, and a high jet of spray shot up out of the hole that God had made.

'Now go on blowing,' said God.

Whale-Wort blew and blew. Soon he was quite a bit smaller. As he shrank, his skin, that had been so tight and glossy, became covered with tiny wrinkles. At last God said to him:

'When you're as small as a cucumber, just give a shout. Then you can come back into my garden. But until then, you shall stay in the sea.'

And God walked away with all his creatures, leaving Whale-Wort rolling and blowing in the sea.

Soon Whale-Wort was down to the size of a bus. But blowing was hard work, and by this time he felt like a sleep. He took a deep breath and sank down to the bottom of the sea for a sleep. Above all, he loved to sleep.

When he awoke he gave a roar of dismay. While he was asleep he had grown back to the length of a street and the fatness of a ship with two funnels.

He rose to the surface as fast as he could and began to blow. Soon he was back down to the size of a lorry. But, soon, too, he felt like another sleep. He took a deep breath and sank to the bottom.

When he awoke he was back to the length of a street.

This went on for years. It is still going on.

As fast as Whale-Wort shrinks with blowing, he grows with sleeping. Sometimes, when he is feeling very strong, he gets himself down to the size of a motor-car. But always, before he gets himself down to the size of a cucumber, he remembers how nice it is to sleep. When he wakes, he has grown again.

He longs to come back on land and sleep in the sun, with his root in the earth. But instead of that, he must roll and blow, out on the wild sea. And until he is allowed to come back on land, the creatures call him just Whale.

HOW the FOX CAME TO BE WHERE IT IS

NOW THERE WERE TWO creatures that were very much alike. Only one was rusty-red, with a thick tail, neat legs, and black pricking ears, while the other was just plain shaggy black-and-white. They were both rivals for the job of guarding Man's farm from the other animals.

The shaggy black-and-white one was called Foursquare, and he wanted the job because he longed to lie beside Man's fire on the cold nights. The rusty-red one was called Slylooking, and he wanted the job for a very different reason. He loved cabbages, and the only way to get near Man's cabbages was by pretending to guard them.

This rivalry went on for a long time, and still neither of them had got the job. At last Man told them to settle the matter between themselves, within a week, or else he would have to employ a bird.

'It is plain,' said Slylooking, 'that we must put our problem before a committee.'

'Very well,' said Foursquare. 'I'm glad to see you so fair-minded. I suggest that we let the cows decide it. They ponder a great deal.'

'But about what?' cried Slylooking, pretending to be alarmed. 'Scenery! That's what they ponder about. They gaze at the scenery and it looks as if they're pondering, and so they get a great name as thinkers. They're no use for important, deep problems such as ours.'

'Then whom do you suggest?'

Now Slylooking had a secret plan. 'I suggest,' he said with a sly look, 'I suggest the hens. They sit on their perches, without a move, and in the dark and all night long – they have nothing else to do but think. They have no scenery to distract them. Besides, they have a fine chairman, the cock, who keeps them in very good order.'

'Then hens it is,' said Foursquare generously.

The hens listened carefully to the problem and promised to give their answer by eleven o'clock next morning.

Foursquare found a soft warm place between hayricks and settled down for the night. But Slylooking could not sleep. He had much too much to do.

First of all he went to Rabbit-Becomer. He said that he had discovered a whole store of cabbages which, he knew, Rabbit loved as much as he himself did.

'Where? Where?' cried Rabbit, hopping from one leg to the other.

'Well,' said Slylooking with a sly look, 'they're in the garden inside Man's farm. If only I could dig a hole as well as you can, I'd have them in a jiffy. Now if you…'

His voice sank to a whisper.

Away went Rabbit with Slylooking to dig the hole. After an hour's hard digging, under Slylooking's directions, Rabbit burst up through the floor of the hen-house. In a flash, Slylooking slipped past him. The hens shouted and flapped in the darkness for a moment — then snickity-snackity! Fox had gobbled the lot.

'These are lively cabbages,' said Rabbit, blinking in the darkness.

'They're the wrong ones!' cried Slylooking, pretending to be very alarmed. 'Run for your life, they don't taste like cabbages at all. I think they're cocks and hens.'

At this, rabbit ran, and behind him, laughing silently, ran Slylooking, away down the long burrow.

Next morning Slylooking roused Foursquare, and together they went along to the hen-house to hear the decision. Slylooking kept his head turned so that Foursquare should not see him smile. He knocked loudly on the hen-house door. When there was no answer, he pretended to look very surprised.

'They must be still deep in thought,' he said, as he knocked again. Still there was no answer, and with a puzzled frown at Foursquare, he opened the door.

And immediately jumped back.

'Murder! Murder!' he cried. 'Oh, look at the poor hens!'

Foursquare ran in. Nothing was to be seen but piles of feathers and a fresh rabbit hole in the middle of the floor.

'Who's been here?' cried Slylooking, pointing at the burrow.

'Well, that looks like Rabbit's work,' said Foursquare.

'The villain!' cried Slylooking. 'Does he hope to get away with this?'

And away he went down the long burrow, almost choking with laughter.

He found Rabbit crouched in the end of a side-shoot, still trembling, terrified by what Slylooking had persuaded him to do. Without a word, Slylooking bundled him into a sack and carried him back to Man.

'Here's the villain who murdered all your poor chickens,' he said. 'Put him in your pot.'

Man was delighted. He was so pleased, in fact, that he employed Slylooking on the spot to guard his farm, and told him to go and tell Foursquare the decision.

And so Slylooking became the sentry at the farm and was happy among the cabbages. But not for long. He could not get out of his head the way those hens had tasted. One night, as he patrolled the farm, chewing a cabbage leaf, he thought and thought of those hens until he could bear it no longer. There were new hens in the hen-house and Slylooking went straight there.

'Good evening, ladies,' he said as he entered. 'Is everything all right?' Once he had the door closed behind him he chose the fattest hen and snap! she was gone. The others looked at him in alarm.

'What will Man say when we tell him?' they cried.

Slylooking smiled, and snuppity, snippity, snoppity, snap! There was nothing left but a pile of feathers.

Next morning, Man just couldn't understand it. But he put new hens in the hen-house. Slylooking swore he had never heard a thing.

That night he visited the hen-house again.

And so every night for a week. He couldn't resist it. And each time he had to gobble up every single hen lest any be left to tell Man what he had been up to. He quite lost his taste for cabbage leaves.

One evening, as he was going for a stroll in the fields, he met Foursquare.

'What are you doing, still snooping round here? Away with you!' he cried. 'I've to guard the farm against such creatures as you.'

Foursquare looked at him steadily and said, 'You have a hen feather in the corner of your mouth.'

Slylooking was furious, but before he could say anything Foursquare had walked away.

Slylooking didn't like Foursquare's remark at all. It looked as if he suspected the truth. So Slylooking decided to play a trick on Foursquare and get rid of him. He went straight to Man.

'I have an idea,' he said, with a sly look, 'that Foursquare is at the bottom of this hen mystery. He is taking his revenge on you for employing me instead of him.'

'Why,' said Man, 'that seems very likely. Certainly he has very fierce teeth. But how are we to catch him?'

'Leave it to me,' said Slylooking. He had another plan already worked out.

Away he went, and finally he found Foursquare sitting on a green hill watching the river.

'Someone is still eating Man's hens,' said Slylooking. 'Will you help us to catch him?'

Now Foursquare was a very honest creature, and when he heard this he was quite ready to believe that Slylooking was not the culprit as he had suspected.

'How are we to do it?' he asked.

'Well,' said Slylooking, 'it isn't clear whether the murderer comes up through the floor of the hen-house, or whether he comes over the farmyard gate and in at the hen-house door. So tonight, while I watch the farm gate, I want you to hide in the hen-house and keep an eye on the floor.'

'Well, that should catch him, whoever it is,' said Foursquare. 'What time shall I come?'

'Come about midnight. I'll let you in,' said Slylooking with a sly look.

A quarter of an hour before midnight Slylooking slipped into the hen-house and had a banquet of hens.

Then he went off to meet Foursquare. Foursquare was waiting under the hedge.

'Quickly, quickly!' said Slylooking. 'The murderer may be here any minute. Hurry. Into the hen-house.'

As soon as Foursquare was in the hen-house with the pile of feathers, Slylooking bolted the door and ran for Man.

'I've trapped the murderer!' he cried. 'I've got him!'

Man came running to see who it was.

'Why, it's Foursquare. Just as you said. Well done, Slylooking.' Man dragged Foursquare out of the hen-house, tied him to the fence, and ran to fetch his gun.

Slylooking danced round poor Foursquare, looking at him merrily out of his eye-corner and singing:

> 'This is the end of this stor-ee,
> Bullets for you and chickens for me.'

'Oh, is that so!' roared Man's voice. He had returned more quickly than Slylooking had expected. Bang! went his gun, and Bang! But Slylooking was over the wall and three fields away and still running.

There and then Man untied Foursquare and led him into the farm kitchen. He gave him a great bowlful of food and after that a rug to stretch out on at the fireside.

But that night, and every night after it, Slylooking had to sleep in the wet wood. And whenever he came sneaking back to the farm, sniffing for hens, Foursquare would hear him. He would jump up from his rug, barking at the top of his voice, and Man would be out through the door with his gun.

But Slylooking was too foxy to be caught. In fact, he was so foxy that pretty soon nobody called him Slylooking any more. They called him what we call him – plain Fox.

HOW
THE POLAR
BEAR
BECAME

WHEN THE ANIMALS HAD been on earth for some time they grew tired of admiring the trees, the flowers, and the sun. They began to admire each other. Every animal was eager to be admired, and spent a part of each day making itself look more beautiful.

Soon they began to hold beauty contests.

Sometimes Tiger won the prize, sometimes Eagle, and sometimes Ladybird. Every animal tried hard.

One animal in particular won the prize almost every time. This was Polar Bear.

Polar Bear was white. Not quite snowy white, but much whiter than any of the other creatures. Everyone admired her. In secret, too, everyone was envious of her. But however much they wished that she wasn't quite so beautiful, they couldn't help giving her the prize.

'Polar Bear,' they said, 'with your white fur, you are almost too beautiful.'

All this went to Polar Bear's head. In fact, she became vain. She was always washing and polishing her fur, trying to make it still whiter. After a while she was winning the prize every time. The only times any other creature got a chance to win was when it rained. On those days Polar Bear would say:

'I shall not go out in the wet. The other creatures will be muddy, and my white fur may get splashed.'

Then, perhaps, Frog or Duck would win for a change.

She had a crowd of young admirers who were always hanging around her cave. They were mainly Seals, all very giddy. Whenever she came out they made a loud shrieking roar:

'Ooooooh! How beautiful she is!'

Before long, her white fur was more important to Polar Bear than anything. Whenever a single speck of dust landed on the tip of one hair of it – she was furious.

'How can I be expected to keep beautiful in this country!' she cried then. 'None of you have ever seen me at my best, because of the dirt here. I am really much whiter than any of you have ever seen me. I think I shall have to go into another country. A country where there is none of this dust. Which country would be best?'

She used to talk in this way because then the Seals would cry:

'Oh, please don't leave us. Please don't take your beauty away from us. We will do anything for you.'

And she loved to hear this.

Soon animals were coming from all over the world to look at her. They stared and stared as Polar Bear stretched out on her rock in the sun. Then they went off home and tried to make themselves look like her. But it was no use. They were all the wrong colour. They were black, or brown, or yellow, or ginger, or fawn, or speckled, but not one of them was white. Soon most of them gave up trying to look beautiful. But they still came every day to gaze enviously at Polar Bear. Some brought picnics. They sat in a vast crowd among the trees in front of her cave.

'Just look at her,' said Mother Hippo to her children. 'Now see that you grow up like that.'

But nothing pleased Polar Bear.

'The dust these crowds raise!' she sighed. 'Why can't I ever get away from them? If only there were some spotless, shining country, all for me...'

Now pretty well all the creatures were tired of her being so much more admired than they were. But one creature more so than the rest. He was Peregrine Falcon.

He was a beautiful bird, all right. But he was not white. Time and again, in the beauty contest he was runner-up to Polar Bear.

'If it were not for her,' he raged to himself, 'I should be first every time.'

He thought and thought for a plan to get rid of her. How? How? How? At last he had it.

One day he went up to Polar Bear.

Now Peregrine Falcon had been to every country in the world. He was a great traveller, as all the creatures well knew.

'I know a country,' he said to Polar Bear, 'which is so clean it is even whiter than you are. Yes, yes, I know, you are beautifully white, but this country is even whiter. The rocks are clear glass and the earth is frozen ice-cream. There is no dirt there, no dust, no mud. You would become whiter than ever in that country. And no one lives there. You could be queen of it.'

Polar Bear tried to hide her excitement.

'I could be queen of it, you say?' she cried. 'This country sounds made for me. No crowds, no dirt? And the rocks, you say, are glass?'

'The rocks,' said Peregrine Falcon, 'are mirrors.'

'Wonderful!' cried Polar Bear.

'And the rain,' he said, 'is white face powder.'

'Better than ever!' she cried. 'How quickly can I be there, away from all these staring crowds and all this dirt?'

'I am going to another country,' she told the other animals. 'It is too dirty here to live.'

Peregrine Falcon hired Whale to carry his passenger. He sat on Whale's forehead, calling out the directions. Polar Bear sat on the shoulder, gazing at the sea. The Seals, who had begged to go with her, sat on the tail.

After some days, they came to the North Pole, where it is all snow and ice.

'Here you are,' cried Peregrine Falcon. 'Everything just as I said. No crowds, no dirt, nothing but beautiful clean whiteness.'

'And the rocks actually are mirrors!' cried Polar Bear,
and she ran to the nearest iceberg to repair her beauty after
the long trip.

Every day now, she sat on one iceberg or another, making
herself beautiful in the mirror of the ice. Always, near her,
sat the Seals. Her fur became whiter and whiter in this new
clean country. And as it became whiter, the Seals praised
her beauty more and more. When she herself saw the
improvement in her looks she said:

'I shall never go back to that dirty old country again.'

And there she is still, with all her admirers around her.

Peregrine Falcon flew back to the other creatures and
told them that Polar Bear had gone for ever. They were all
very glad, and set about making themselves beautiful at once.
Every single one was saying to himself:

'Now that Polar Bear is out of the way, perhaps I shall
have a chance of the prize at the beauty contest.'

And Peregrine Falcon was saying to himself:

'Surely, now, I am the most beautiful of all creatures.'

But that first contest was won by Little Brown Mouse
for her pink feet.

HOW the HYENA
BECAME

ONE CREATURE, a Wild-Dog-Becomer called Hyena, copied Leopard-Becomer in everything he did.

Leopard-Becomer was already one of the most respected creatures on the plains. He was strong, swift, fierce, graceful, and had the most beautiful spotted skin.

Hyena longed to be like this. He practised walking like him, crouching like him, pouncing like him. He studied his every move. 'I must get it perfect,' he kept saying to himself.

He followed Leopard-Becomer so closely, in fact, that he never had time to go off and kill his own game. So he had to eat what Leopard left. Leopard didn't take at all kindly to Hyena, and often made him wait a long time for the left-overs. In this way Hyena grew used to eating meat that was none too fresh.

Nevertheless, so long as he could keep near Leopard he was satisfied.

Only one thing could take him from Leopard's track, and that was a chance to boast to the wild-dogs.

'You're nothing but a Wild-Dog yourself,' they said. 'Who do you think you are? Putting on all these Leopard airs?'

'Ha ha,' he replied. 'You wait. Watch me and wait. You're in for a surprise. I'll be a leopard yet.'

One morning he awoke to find his skin covered with big spots, almost like a leopard's.

'Joy! Joy!' he cried, and danced about till he was sodden with dew. He ran off to show himself to the wild-dogs. When they saw his spots they all fled, looking back over their shoulders fearfully.

'Ha ha!' cried Hyena. 'So you thought I was Leopard, did you?'

It was a long time before he could persuade them that he really was Hyena. Even so, they never quite trusted him again.

They began to move away quietly whenever they saw him coming.

As for Hyena, he returned to his Leopard-Becoming with a renewed zest.

This went on for many years.

At last, Hyena began to feel impatient.

'Shall I never be a leopard?' he asked himself. 'I'm still not anywhere near as good as Leopard-Becomer. In fact, he picks up new tricks faster than I learn his old ones.'

He ran to the Wild-Dog-Becomers.

'Am I Leopard yet?' he asked.

They peeped back over the skyline behind which they had run at the first sight of him.

'You are not,' they said. 'But you are not Wild-Dog either, not any more. The Lord knows what sort of a thing you are now.'

Hyena went back to Leopard. For some years he went about in a very disgruntled condition, but still following Leopard. One day he came as close to Leopard as he dared and said:

'Shall I never become a leopard, Leopard?'

Leopard looked at him in disgust.

'You,' he said, 'have already become what you are going to become.'

'And what is that, please?' asked Hyena politely.

'You have become,' said Leopard, 'a Leopard-Follower.'

Hyena retired to a safe distance and thought about this. He became very embittered.

'Very well,' he said at last. 'If I cannot ever be a leopard, that's finished it. I shall go back to being a wild-dog. Leopard is a stupid creature anyway, calling me a Leopard-Follower.'

And he ran back to the wild-dogs. He knew they would run away when they caught sight of him, so while he was still in the distance he began to shout:

'It's me, Hyena. I'm coming back to be one of you. I've finished with Leopard.'

But it was no use. The wild-dogs ran, and faster than Hyena they ran. He chased them as far as he could move, shouting till his throat ached. At last he stood alone, panting, in the middle of a flat, empty, silent plain.

Sadly, he drooped his tail and turned back. He was feeling hungry. Then he remembered that he didn't know how to kill anything. He walked on and on, getting hungrier and hungrier.

Suddenly he stopped, and sniffed. A leopard had killed a gazelle near there a week ago. He found the bones, cracked them, and sucked them. Then, sniffing, he followed the track of the leopard.

This leopard lived under a rock on top of a hill. Hyena made his bed at the bottom of the hill. Whenever Leopard went out hunting Hyena followed him and ate what he left. In this way he lived.

But he was deeply ashamed. He now saw that he was nothing but a Leopard-Follower after all. He became more bitter than ever. He no longer imitated Leopard. His greatest pleasure now was to sit at a safe distance, when Leopard was eating, and make critical remarks in a loud clear voice:

'What a stupid animal you are! How gluttonously you eat! How boorishly you tear the meat! How disgustingly you growl as you chew!'

And between each comment he gave a laugh, a loud mocking laugh, so that all the other animals within hearing would think he was getting the better of Leopard in some way.

'If I cannot be a leopard,' he said to himself, 'then you shall be ashamed of being a leopard.'

Leopard, of course, was much too fine a beast ever to be ashamed of being what he was.

That was as far as Hyena ever got. He is the same still. He follows Leopard from meal to meal, and laughs and laughs, while Leopard gorges himself on the choicest portions of the meat.

Afterwards, when Leopard has eaten his fill and strolled off to sleep, Hyena stops laughing. Then, at dusk, and on bent legs so as not to be seen, he runs in and tears and gulps all night long at the bones and scraps and rags of meat that are left.

HOW THE TORTOISE
BECAME

WHEN GOD MADE A CREATURE, he first of all shaped it in clay. Then he baked it in the ovens of the sun until it was hard. Then he took it out of the oven and, when it was cool, breathed life into it. Last of all, he pulled its skin on to it like a tight jersey.

All the animals got different skins. If it was a cold day, God would give to the animals he made on that day a dense, woolly skin. Snow was falling heavily when he made the sheep and the bears.

If it was a hot day, the new animals got a thin skin. On the day he made greyhounds and dachshunds and boys and girls, the weather was so hot God had to wear a sun hat and was calling endlessly for iced drinks.

Now on the day he made Torto, God was so hot the sweat was running down on to the tips of his fingers.

After baking Torto in the oven, God took him out to cool. Then he flopped back in his chair and ordered Elephant to fan him with its ears. He had made Elephant only a few days before and was very pleased with its big flapping ears. At last he thought that Torto must surely be cool.

'He's had as long as I usually give a little thing like him,' he said, and picking up Torto, he breathed life into him. As he did so, he found out his mistake.

Torto was not cool. Far from it. On that hot day, with no cooling breezes, Torto had remained scorching hot. Just as he was when he came out of the oven.

'Ow!' roared God. He dropped Torto and went hopping away on one leg to the other end of his workshop, shaking his burnt fingers.

'Ow, ow, ow!' he roared again, and plunged his hand into a dish of butter to cure the burns.

Torto meanwhile lay on the floor, just alive, groaning with the heat.

'Oh, I'm so hot!' he moaned. 'So hot! The heat. Oh, the heat!'

God was alarmed that he had given Torto life before he was properly cooled.

'Just a minute, Torto,' he said. 'I'll have a nice, thin, cooling skin on you in a jiffy. Then you'll feel better.'

But Torto wanted no skin. He was too hot as it was.

'No, no!' he cried. 'I shall stifle. Let me go without a skin for a few days. Let me cool off first.'

'That's impossible,' said God. 'All creatures must have skins.'

'No, no!' cried Torto, wiping the sweat from his little brow. 'No skin!'

'Yes!' cried God.

'No!' cried Torto.

'Yes!'

'No!'

God made a grab at Torto, who ducked and ran like lightning under a cupboard. Without any skin to cumber his movements, Torto felt very light and agile.

'Come out!' roared God, and got down on his knees to grope under the cupboard for Torto.

In a flash, Torto was out from under the other end of the cupboard, and while God was still struggling to his feet, he ran out through the door and into the world, without a skin.

The first thing he did was to go to a cool pond and plunge straight into it. There he lay, for several days, just cooling off. Then he came out and began to live among the other creatures. But he was still very hot. Whenever he felt his own heat getting too much for him, he retired to his pond to cool off in the water. In this way, he found life pleasant enough.

Except for one thing. The other creatures didn't approve of Torto.

They all had skins. When they saw Torto without a skin, they were horrified.

'But he has no skin!' cried Porcupine.

'It's disgusting!' cried Yak. 'It's indecent!'

'He's not normal. Leave him to himself,' said Sloth.

So all the animals began to ignore Torto. But they couldn't ignore him completely, because he was a wonderfully swift runner, and whenever they held a race, he won it. He was so nimble without a skin that none of the other creatures could hope to keep up with him.

'I'm a genius-runner,' he said. 'You should respect me. I am faster than the lot of you put together. I was made different.'

But the animals still ignored him. Even when they had to give him the prizes for winning all the races, they still ignored him.

'Torto is a very swift mover,' they said. 'And perhaps swifter than any of us. But what sort of a creature is he? No skin!'

And they all turned up their noses.

At first, Torto didn't care at all. When the animals collected together, with all their fur brushed and combed and set neatly, he strolled among them, smiling happily, naked.

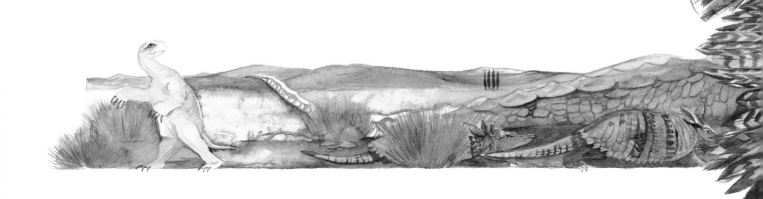

'When will this disgusting creature learn to behave?' cried Turkey, loudly enough for everyone to hear.

'Just take no notice of him,' said Alligator, and lumbered round, in his heavy armour, to face in the opposite direction.

All the animals turned round to face in the opposite direction.

When Torto went up to Grizzly Bear to ask what everyone was looking at, Grizzly Bear pretended to have a fly in his ear. When he went to Armadillo, Armadillo gathered up all his sons and daughters and led them off without a word or a look.

'So that's your game, is it?' said Torto to himself. Then aloud, he said: 'Never mind. Wait till it comes to the races.'

When the races came, later in the afternoon, Torto won them all. But nobody cheered. He collected the prizes and went off to his pond alone.

'They're jealous of me,' he said. 'That's why they ignore me. But I'll punish them: I'll go on winning all the races.'

That night, God came to Torto and begged him to take a proper skin before it was too late. Torto shook his head:

'The other animals are snobs,' he said. 'Just because they are covered with a skin, they think everyone else should be covered with one too. That's snobbery. But I shall teach them not to be snobs by making them respect me. I shall go on winning all the races.'

And so he did. But still the animals didn't respect him. In fact, they grew to dislike him more and more.

One day there was a very important race-meeting, and all the animals collected at the usual place. But the minute Torto arrived they simply walked away. Simply got up and walked away. Torto sat on the race-track and stared after them. He felt really left out.

'Perhaps,' he thought sadly, 'it would be better if I had a skin. I mightn't be able to run then, but at least I would have friends. I have no friends. Besides, after all this practice, I would still be able to run quite fast.'

But as soon as he said that he felt angry with himself.

'No!' he cried. 'They are snobs. I shall go on winning their races in spite of them. I shall teach them a lesson.'

And he got up from where he was sitting and followed them. He found them all in one place, under a tree. And the races were being run.

'Hey!' he called as he came up to them 'What about me?'

But at that moment, Tiger held up a sign in front of him. On the sign, Torto read: 'Creatures without skins are not allowed to enter.'

Torto went home and brooded. God came up to him.

'Well, Torto,' said God kindly, 'would you like a skin yet?'

Torto thought deeply.

'Yes,' he said at last, 'I would like a skin. But only a very special sort of skin.'

'And what sort of a skin is that?' asked God.

'I would like,' said Torto, 'a skin that I can put on, or take off, just whenever I please.'

God frowned.

'I'm afraid,' he said, 'I have none like that.'

'Then make one,' replied Torto. 'You're God.'

God went away and came back within an hour.

'Do you want a beautiful skin?' he asked. 'Or do you mind if it's very ugly?'

'I don't care what sort of a skin it is,' said Torto, 'so long as I can take it off and put it back on again just whenever I please.'

God went away again, and again came back within an hour.

'Here it is. That's the best I can do.'

'What's this!' cried Torto. 'But it's horrible!'

'Take it or leave it,' said God, and walked away.

Torto examined the skin. It was tough, rough, and stiff.

'It's like a coconut,' he said. 'With holes in it.'

And so it was. Only it was shiny. When he tried it on, he found it quite snug. It had only one disadvantage. He could move only very slowly in it.

'What's the hurry?' he said to himself then. 'When it comes to moving, who can move faster than me?'

And he laughed. Suddenly he felt delighted. Away he went to where the animals were still running their races.

As he came near to them, he began to think that perhaps his skin was a little rough and ready. But he checked himself:

'Why should I dress up for them?' he said. 'This rough old thing will do. The races are the important thing.'

Tiger lowered his notice and stared in dismay as Torto swaggered past him. All the animals were now turning and staring, nudging each other, and turning, and staring.

'That's a change, anyway,' thought Torto.

Then, as usual, he entered for all the races.

The animals began to talk and laugh among themselves as they pictured Torto trying to run in his heavy new clumsy skin.

'He'll look silly, and then how we'll laugh.' And they all laughed.

But when he took his skin off at the starting-post, their laughs turned to frowns.

He won all the races, then climbed back into his skin to collect the prizes. He strutted in front of all the animals.

'Now it's my turn to be snobbish,' he said to himself.

Then he went home, took off his skin, and slept sweetly. Life was perfect for him.

This went on for many years. But though the animals would now speak to him, they remembered what he had been. That didn't worry Torto, however. He became very fond of his skin. He began to keep it on at night when he came home after the races. He began to do everything in it, except actually race. He crept around slowly, smiling at the leaves, letting the days pass.

There came a time when there were no races for several weeks. During all this time Torto never took his skin off once. Until, when the first race came round at last, he found he could not take his skin off at all, no matter how he pushed and pulled. He was stuck inside it. He strained and squeezed and gasped, but it was no use. He was stuck.

However, he had already entered for all the races, so he had to run.

He lined up, in his skin, at the start, alongside Hare, Greyhound, Cheetah and Ostrich. They were all great runners, but usually he could beat the lot of them easily. The crowd stood agog.

'Perhaps,' Torto was thinking, 'my skin won't make much difference. I've never really tried to run my very fastest in it.'

The starter's pistol cracked, and away went Greyhound, Hare, Cheetah and Ostrich, neck and neck. Where was Torto?

The crowed roared with laughter.

Torto had fallen on his face and had not moved an inch. At his first step, cumbered by his stiff, heavy skin, he had fallen on his face. But he tried. He climbed back on to his feet and made one stride, slowly, then a second stride, and was just about to make a third when the race was over and Cheetah had won. Torto had moved not quite three paces. How the crowd laughed!

And so it was with all the races. In not one race did Torto manage to make more than three steps, before it was over.

The crowd was enjoying itself. Torto was weeping with shame.

After the last race, he turned to crawl home. He only wanted to hide. But though the other animals had let him go off alone when he had the prizes, now they came alongside him, in a laughing, mocking crowd.

'Who's the slowest of all the creatures?' they shouted.

'Torto is!'

'Who's the slowest of all the creatures?'

'Torto is' — all the way home.

After that, Torto tried to keep himself out of sight, but the other animals never let him rest. Whenever any of them chanced to see him, they would shout at the tops of their voices:

'Who's the slowest of all the creatures?'

And every other creature within hearing would answer, at the tops of their voices:

'Torto is!'

And that is how Torto came to be known as 'Tortoise'.

HOW the BEE
BECAME

NOW IN THE MIDDLE of the earth lived a demon. This demon spent all his time groping about in the dark tunnels, searching for precious metals and gems.

He was hunch-backed and knobbly-armed. His ears draped over his shoulders like a wrinkly cloak. These kept him safe from the bits of rock that were always falling from the ceilings of his caves. He had only one eye, which was a fire. To keep this fire alive he had to feed it with gold and silver. Over this eye he cooked his supper every night. It is hard to say what he ate. All kinds of fungus that grew in the airless dark on the rocks. His drink was mostly tar and oil, which he loved. There is no end of tar and oil in the middle of the earth.

He rarely came up to the light. Once, when he did, he saw the creatures that God was making.

'What's this?' he cried, when a grasshopper landed on his clawed, horny foot. Then he saw Lion. Then Cobra. Then, far above him, Eagle.

'My word!' he said, and hurried back down into his dark cave to think about what he had seen.

He was jealous of the beautiful things that God was making.

'I will make something,' he said at last, 'which will be far more beautiful than any of God's creatures.'

But he had no idea how to set about it.

So one day he crept up to God's workshop and watched God at work. He peeped from behind the door. He saw him model the clay, bake it in the sun's fire, then breathe life into it. So that was it!

Away he dived, back down into the centre of the earth.

At the centre of the earth it was too hot for clay. Everything was already baked hard. He set about trying to make his own clay.

First, he ground up stones between his palms. That was powder. But how was he to make it into clay? He needed water, and there in the centre of the earth it was too hot for water.

He searched and he searched, but there was none. At last he sat down. He felt so sad he began to cry. Big tears rolled down his nose.

'If only I had water,' he sobbed, 'this clay could become a real living creature. Why do I have to live where there is no water?'

He looked at the powder in his palm, and began to cry afresh. As he looked and wept, and looked and wept, a tear fell off the end of his nose straight into the powder.

But he was too late. A demon's tears are no ordinary tears. There was a red flash, a fizz, a bubbling, and where the powder had been was nothing but a dark stain on his palm.

He felt like weeping again. Now he had water, but no powder.

'So much for stone-powder,' he said. 'I need something stronger.'

Then quickly, before his tears dried, he ground some of the precious metal that he used to feed the fire of his eye. As soon as it was powder he wetted it with a tear off his cheek. But it was no better than the stone-powder had been. There was a flash, a fizz, a bubbling, and nothing.

'Well,' he said. 'What now?'

At last he thought of it – he would make a powder of precious gems. It was hard work grinding these, but at last he had finished. Now for a tear. But he was too excited to cry. He struggled to bring up a single tear. It was no good. His eye was dry as an oven. He struggled and he struggled. Nothing! All at once he sat down and burst into tears.

'It's no good!' he cried. 'I can't cry!' Then he felt his tears wet on his cheeks.

'I'm crying!' he cried joyfully. 'Quick, quick!' And he splashed a tear on to the powder of the precious gems.
The result was perfect. He had made a tiny piece of beautiful clay. Only tiny, because his tears had been few. But it was big enough.

'Now,' he said, 'what kind of creature shall I make?'

The jewel-clay was very hard to work into shape. It was tough as red-hot iron.

So he laid the clay on his anvil and began to beat it into shape with his great hammer.

He beat and beat and beat that clay for a thousand years.

And at last it was shaped. Now it needed baking. Very carefully, because the thing he had made was very frail, he put it into the fire of his eye to bake.

Then, beside a great heap of small pieces of gold and silver, for another thousand years he sat, feeding the fire of his eye with the precious metal. All this time, in the depths of his eye glowed his little creature, baking slowly.

At last it was baked.

Now came the real problem. How was he going to breathe life into it?

He puffed and he blew, but it was no good.

'It is so beautiful!' he cried. 'I must give it life!'

It certainly was beautiful. All the precious gems of which it was made mingled their colours. And from the flames in which it had been baked, it had taken a dark fire. It gleamed and flashed: red, blue, orange, green, purple, no bigger than your finger-nail.

But it had no life.

There was only one thing to do. He must go to God and ask him to breathe life into it.

When God saw the demon he was amazed. He had no idea that such a creature existed.

'Who are you?' he asked. 'Where have you come from?'

The demon hung his head. 'Now,' he thought, 'I will use a trick.'

'I'm a jewel-smith,' he said humbly. 'And I live in the centre of the earth. I have brought you a present, to show my respect for you.'

He showed God the little creature that he had made. God was amazed again.

'How beautiful!' he kept saying as he turned it over on his hand. 'How beautiful! What a wonderfully clever smith you are.'

'Ah!' said the demon. 'But not so clever as you. I could never breathe life into it. If you had made it, it would be alive. As it is, it is beautiful, but dead.'

God was flattered. 'That's soon altered,' he said. He raised the demon's gift to his lips and breathed life into it.

Then he held it out. It crawled on to the end of his finger.

'Buzz!' it went, and whirred its thin, beautiful wings. Like a flash, the demon snatched it from God's finger-tip and plunged back down into the centre of the earth.

There, for another thousand years, he lay, letting the little creature crawl over his fingers and make short flights from one hand to the other. It glittered all its colours in the light of his eye's fire. The demon was very happy.

'You are more beautiful than any of God's creatures,' he crooned.

But life was hard for the little creature down in the centre of the earth, with no one to play with but the demon. He had God's breath in him, and he longed to be among the other creatures under the sun.

And he was sad for another reason. In his veins ran not blood, but the tears with which the demon had mixed his clay. And what is sadder than a tear? Feeling the sadness in all his veins, he moved restlessly over the demon's hands.

One day the demon went up to the light to compare his little creature with the ones God had made.

'Buzz!' went his pet, and was away over a mountain.

'Come back!' roared the demon, then quickly covered his mouth with his hands, frightened that God would hear him. He began to search for his creature, but soon, frightened that God would see him, he crept back into the earth.

Still his little creature was not happy.

The sadness of the demon's tears was always in him. It was part of him. It was what flowed in his veins.

'If I gather everything that is sweet and bright and happy,' he said to himself, 'that should make me feel better. Here there are plenty of wonderfully sweet bright happy things.'

And he began to fly from flower to flower, collecting the bright sunny sweetness out of their cups.

'Ah!' he cried. 'Wonderful!'

The sweetness lit up his body. He felt the sun glowing through him from what he drank. For the first time in his life he felt happy.

But the moment he stopped drinking from the flowers, the sadness came creeping back along his veins and the gloom into his thoughts.

'That demon made me of tears,' he said. 'How can I ever hope to get away from the sadness of tears? Unless I never leave these flowers.'

And he hurried from flower to flower.

He could never stop, and it was too good to stop.

Soon, he had drunk so much, the sweetness began to ooze out of his pores. He was so full of it, he was brimming over with it. And every second he drank more.

At last he had to pause.

'I must store all this somewhere,' he said.

So he made a hive, and all the sweetness that oozed from him he stored in that hive. Man found it and called it honey. God saw what the little creature was doing, and blessed him, and called him Bee.

But Bee must still go from flower to flower, seeking sweetness. The tears of the demon are still in his veins ready to make him gloomy the moment he stops drinking from the flowers. When he is angry and stings, the smart of his sting is the tear of the demon. If he has to keep that sweet, it is no wonder that he drinks sweetness until he brims over.

HOW the CAT BECAME

THINGS WERE RUNNING VERY SMOOTHLY and most of the creatures were highly pleased with themselves. Lion was already famous. Even the little shrews and moles and spiders were pretty well known.

But among all these busy creatures there was one who seemed to be getting nowhere. It was Cat.

Cat was a real oddity. The others didn't know what to make of him at all.

He lived in a hollow tree in the wood. Every night, when the rest of the creatures were sound asleep, he retired to the depths of his tree – then such sounds, such screechings, yowlings, wailings! The bats that slept upside-down all day long in the hollows of the tree branches awoke with a start and fled with their wing-tips stuffed into their ears. It seemed to them that Cat was having the worst nightmares ever – ten at a time.

But no. Cat was tuning his violin.

If only you could have seen him! Curled in the warm smooth hollow of his tree, gazing up through the hole at the top of the trunk, smiling at the stars, winking at the moon – his violin tucked under his chin. Ah, Cat was a happy one.

And all night long he sat there composing his tunes.

Now the creatures didn't like this at all. They saw no use in his music, it made no food, it built no nest, it didn't even keep him warm. And the way Cat lounged around all day, sleeping in the sun, was just more than they could stand.

'He's a bad example,' said Beaver, 'he never does a stroke of work! What if our children think they can live as idly as he does?'

'It's time,' said Weasel, 'that Cat had a job like everybody else in the world.'

So the creatures of the wood formed a Committee to persuade Cat to take a job.

Jay, Magpie, and Parrot went along at dawn and sat in the topmost twigs of Cat's old tree. As soon as Cat poked his head out, they all began together:

'You've to get a job. Get a job! Get a job!'

That was only the beginning of it. All day long, everywhere he went, those birds were at him:

'Get a job! Get a job!'

And try as he would, Cat could not get one wink of sleep.

That night he went back to his tree early. He was far too tired to practise on his violin and fell fast asleep in a few minutes. Next morning, when he poked his head out of the tree at first light, the three birds of the Committee were there again, loud as ever:

'Get a job!'

Cat ducked back down into his tree and began to think. He wasn't going to start grubbing around in the wet woods all day, as they wanted him to. Oh no. He wouldn't have any time to play his violin if he did that. There was only one thing to do and he did it.

He tucked his violin under his arm and suddenly jumped out at the top of the tree and set off through the woods at a run. Behind him, shouting and calling, came Jay, Magpie, and Parrot.

Other creatures that were about their daily work in the undergrowth looked up when Cat ran past. No one had ever seen Cat run before.

'Cat's up to something,' they called to each other. 'Maybe he's going to get a job at last.'

Deer, Wild Boar, Bear, Ferret, Mongoose, Porcupine, and a cloud of birds set off after Cat to see where he was going.

After a great deal of running they came to the edge of the forest. There they stopped. As they peered through the leaves they looked sideways at each other and trembled. Ahead of them, across an open field covered with haycocks, was Man's farm.

But Cat wasn't afraid. He went straight on, over the field, and up to Man's door. He raised his paw and banged as hard as he could in the middle of the door.

Man was so surprised to see Cat that at first he just stood, eyes wide, mouth open. No creature ever dared to come on to his fields, let alone knock at his door. Cat spoke first.

'I've come for a job,' he said.

'A job?' asked Man, hardly able to believe his ears.

'Work,' said Cat. 'I want to earn my living.'

Man looked him up and down, then saw his long claws.

'You look as if you'd make a fine rat-catcher,' said Man.

Cat was surprised to hear that. He wondered what it was about him that made him look like a rat-catcher. Still, he wasn't going to miss the chance of a job. So he stuck out his chest and said: 'Been doing it for years.'

'Well then, I've a job for you,' said Man. 'My farm's swarming with rats and mice. They're in my haystacks, they're in my corn sacks, and they're all over the pantry.'

So before Cat knew where he was, he had been signed on as a Rat-and-Mouse-Catcher. His pay was milk, and meat, and a place at the fireside. He slept all day and worked all night.

At first he had a terrible time. The rats pulled his tail, the mice nipped his ears. They climbed on to rafters above him and dropped down – thump! on to him in the dark. They teased the life out of him.

But Cat was a quick learner. At the end of the week he could lay out a dozen rats and twice as many mice within half an hour. If he'd gone on laying them out all night there would pretty soon have been none left, and Cat would

have been out of a job. So he just caught a few each night —
in the first ten minutes or so. Then he retired into the barn
and played his violin till morning. This was just the job he
had been looking for.

Man was delighted with him. And Mrs Man thought he
was beautiful. She took him on to her lap and stroked him for
hours on end. What a life! thought Cat. If only those silly
creatures in the dripping wet woods could see him now!

Well, when the other farmers saw what a fine rat-and-
mouse-catcher Cat was, they all wanted cats too. Soon there
were so many cats that our Cat decided to form a string band.
Oh yes, they were all great violinists. Every night, after
making one pile of rats and another of mice, each cat left his
farm and was away over the fields to a little dark spinney.

Then what tunes! All night long...

Pretty soon lady cats began to arrive. Now, every night,
instead of just music, there was dancing too. And what
dances! If only you could have crept up there and peeped into
the glade from behind a tree and seen the cats dancing — the
glossy furred ladies and the tomcats, some pearly grey, some
ginger red, and all with wonderful green flashing eyes. Up and
down the glade, with the music flying out all over the night.

At dawn they hung their violins in the larch trees, dashed
back to the farms, and pretended they had been working all
night among the rats and mice. They lapped their milk
hungrily, stretched out at the fireside, and fell asleep with
smiles on their faces.

HOW the DONKEY
BECAME

THERE WAS ONE CREATURE that never seemed to change at all. This didn't worry him, though. He hated the thought of becoming any single creature. Oh no, he wanted to become all creatures together, all at once. He used to practise them all in turn – first a lion, then an eagle, then a bull, then a cockatoo, and so on – five minutes each.

He was a strange-looking beast in those days. A kind of no-shape-in-particular. He had legs, sure enough, and eyes and ears and all the rest. But there was something vague about him. He really did look as if he might suddenly turn into anything.

He was called Donkey, which in the language of that time meant 'unable to stick to one thing'.

'You'll never become anything,' the other creatures said, 'until you stick to one thing and that thing alone.'

'Become a lion with us,' the Lion-Becomers said. 'You're so good at lioning it's a pity to waste your time eagling.'

And the eagles said: 'Never mind lioning. You should concentrate on becoming an eagle. You have a gift for it.'

All the different creatures spoke to him in this way, which made him very proud. So proud, in fact, that he became boastful.

'I'm going to be an Everykind,' Donkey cried, kicking up his heels. 'I'm going to be a Lionocerangoutangadinf.'

Half the day he spent on a high exposed part of the plain practising at his creatures where everyone could see him. The other half he spent sleeping in the long grass. 'I'm growing so fast,' he used to say, 'I need all the sleep I can get.'

But Donkey had a secret worry. He had no means of earning his living. He couldn't earn his living as a lion – not when he only practised at lion five minutes a day. He couldn't earn his living as any other creature either – for the same reason.

So he had to beg.

'When you see me grow up into a Lionocerangoutangadinf,' he said, as he begged a mouthful of fish from Otter, 'you'll be glad you helped me when I was only learning.'

And he went off kicking up his heels.

Before long the animals grew tired of his begging. It took them all day to find food enough for themselves. So whenever Donkey came up to them to beg they began to tease him:

'What?' they cried. 'Aren't you the finest, greatest creature in the world yet? What have you been doing with your time?'

This made Donkey furious. He galloped off to a high hill, and there he sat, brooding.

'The trouble is,' he said, 'there's no place among these creatures for somebody with real ambition. But one day — I'll make them stare! I'll be a better lion than a lion, a better eagle than an eagle, and a better kangaroo than kangaroo — and all at the same time. Then they'll be sorry.'

All the same, he wished he could earn his living without having to beg.

As he sat, he heard a long sigh. He looked around. He hadn't noticed that he was so near Man's farm. He looked over the fence and saw Man sitting beside a well, with his head resting in his hands. As he looked, Man gave another sigh.

'What's the matter?' asked Donkey.

Man looked up.

'I'm weary,' he said. 'Drawing water from this well is hard work.'

'Hard?' Donkey cried. 'If it's strength you're wanting, here I am. I'm the strongest creature on these plains.'

'But still not strong enough to draw water,' sighed Man.

'Just watch this.' Donkey marched across, took hold of the long pole that stuck out over the well, and began to drag it round. He had often seen Man doing this, so he knew how. Water gushed out of a pipe on to Man's field of corn.

'Wonderful!' cried Man. 'Wonderful!'

Donkey flattened back his ears and pulled all the harder. Man danced around him, crying:

'You're a marvel. Oh, what I wouldn't give to have you working for me.'

As he said that, Donkey got an idea. He stopped.

'If you'll give me food,' he said, 'I'll do this every day for you.'

'It's a bargain!' said Man.

So Donkey started to work for Man.

Only a little bit each morning, mind you. He still spent most of his day out on the plains practising at all his creatures. The he retired early to sleep in the little shed that Man had made for him — it was dark, out of the wind, and the floor was covered with deep straw. Lovely! There he would lie till it was time for work next morning.

One day Man said to him:

'If you'll work twice as long for me, I'll give you twice as much food.'

Donkey thought:

'Twice as much food means twice as much strength. And if I'm going to be a Lionocerangoutangadinf — well — I shall need all the strength that's going.'

So he agreed to work twice as long.

Next day, Man asked him the same again. Donkey agreed. And the next day, and again Donkey agreed. He was now working from dawn to dusk. But the pile of food that Man gave him at the day's end! Well, after eating it, Donkey could do nothing but lie down in his straw and snore.

After about a week of this he suddenly thought:

'Here I am, being gloriously fed. Getting stronger and stronger. But I never have time to practise at my creatures. How can I hope to become a Lionocerangoutangadinf if I never practise my creatures?'

So what did he do? He couldn't very well practise while he was working. The sight and sound of it would have terrified Man, and Donkey didn't want to lose his job. So he did the only thing he could. He began to practise in his head.

Soon he got to be wonderfully good at this.

He could fancy himself any creature he wished – a mountain goat, for instance, leaping among the clouds from crag to crag, or a salmon, climbing a swift fierce torrent – for hours at a time, all in his head. He would quite forget that he was only walking round a well.

Once or twice Man removed him from the well and set him to draw a plough. But Donkey was so absorbed in practising at his creatures inside his head that he forgot to turn at the end of the furrow. He went ploughing straight on, through the hedge and into the next field. After this, Man never asked him to do anything but walk around the well, and Donkey was quite contented.

So it went on for several years, and Donkey fancied that he was becoming more and more skilful at his creatures. 'I mustn't be in too great a hurry,' he said to himself. 'I want to be better at everything than every other creature – so a little bit more practice won't hurt.'

So he went on. Always staying on with Man for just a little bit more practice inside his head.

'Soon,' he kept saying, 'soon I shall be perfect.'

At last it seemed to Donkey he was nearly perfect. 'A few more days, just a few more days!' Then he would burst out on to the plains, the first Lionocerangoutangadinf. Within three days, perhaps even within two, the animals would crown him their king – he was sure of that. Just as he was thinking these lovely thoughts he heard a sudden cry.

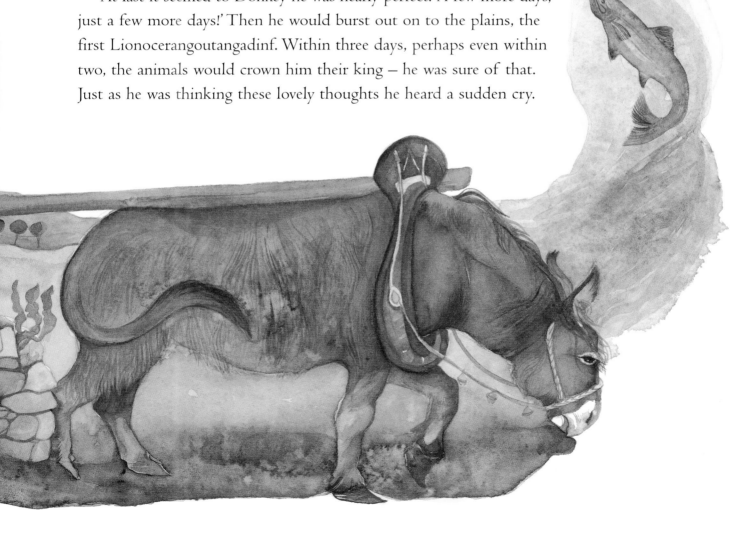

He looked up and saw Man running towards his house, his arms in the air.

At the same moment, over the high fence, came Lion.

Donkey stood, and watched Lion out of the corner of his eye. He tilted one fore-foot carelessly.

Lion stared at him.

At last, making his voice sound as friendly as he could, Donkey said: 'My word, Lion-Becomer, you've changed. Are you Lion yet?'

Lion turned away from him without a word and walked up the path. When he reached Man's house, he stood up on his hind legs and, lifting one paw, like a lion in a coat of arms, began to beat upon the door.

'Throw out your wife and children, Man!' he roared.

Man was crouching under the table inside the house, trembling all over, not daring to breathe.

Finally Lion got tired of beating the door, which was of thick wood and studded with big bolts. He turned round and began to sniff among the outhouses and gardens. He came to Donkey again, who was still propped idly on one fore-leg beside the well.

'Hello again, Lion,' said Donkey, and he let his voice be ever such a little bit scornful. 'Your hunting isn't so good, is it? I think I could give you a lesson or two in lioning.'

Lion stared, amazed.

'Now,' thought Donkey, 'now to reveal my true self. Now to reveal what I have made myself after all these years of hard practice.'

And he gave a great leap and roared.

'See!' he cried. 'This is the way!'

And again he leapt and roared, leapt and roared. He became so taken up with his lioning that he completely forgot about Lion.

Now it was years since Donkey had actually tried to leap or roar. He was far too stiff with his years of hard work to leap, and his voice had become stiff as his muscles.

So, though it seemed to him he was doing a wonderful lion, he was really only kicking out his legs stiffly, and sending up a harsh bray.

But he was delighted with himself. He went on, leaping and roaring, as he thought, leaping and roaring, so that his harness clattered, the long pole bounced and banged, and Lion screwed up his eyes in the dust from the kicking-out feet.

At last Lion could stand it no longer. He raised his paw, and with one blow knocked Donkey clean into the well. He then jumped back over the fence and returned to his wife, who was waiting on the skyline.

Poor Donkey! When Man hauled him out of the well he was in a sorry state. But he was a wiser Donkey. That night he ate his oats and lay down with a new feeling. No more Lionocerangoutangadinf for him. No more pretending to be every creature.

'It's best to face the truth,' he said to himself, 'and the truth is I'm neither a lion nor an eagle. I am a well-fed, comfortable, hard-working Donkey.'

He could hear the lions roaring hungrily out on the plains, and he thought of the antelopes running hither and thither looking for a safe corner and a place out of the wind. He pushed his head under the warm straw, and smiled into the darkness, and fell into a deep sleep.

HOW the HARE
BECAME

OW HARE WAS A REAL DANDY. He was about the vainest creature on the whole earth.

Every morning he spent one hour smartening his fur, another hour smoothing his whiskers, and another cleaning his paws. Then the rest of the day he strutted up and down, admiring his shadow and saying:

'How handsome I am! How amazingly handsome! Surely some great princess will want to marry me soon.'

The other creatures grew so tired of his vain ways that they decided to teach him a lesson. Now they knew that he would believe any story so long as it made him think he was handsome. So this is what they did:

One morning Gazelle went up to Hare and said:

'Good morning, Hare. How handsome you look. No wonder we've been hearing such stories about you.'

'Stories?' asked Hare. 'What stories?'

'Haven't you heard the news?' cried Gazelle. 'It's about you.'

'News? News? What news?' cried Hare, jumping up and down in excitement.

'Why, the moon wants to marry you,' said Gazelle. 'The beautiful moon, the queen of the night sky. She wants to marry you because she says you're the handsomest creature in the whole world. Oh yes. You should just have heard a few of the things she was saying about you last night.'

'Such as?' cried Hare. 'Such as?' He could hardly wait to hear what fine things moon had said about him.

'Never mind now,' said Gazelle. 'But she'll be walking up that hill tonight, and if you want to marry her you're to be there to meet her. Lucky man!'

Gazelle pointed to a hill on the Eastern skyline. It was not yet midday, but Hare was up on top of that hill in one flash, looking down eagerly on the other side. There was no sign of a palace anywhere, where the moon might live. He could see nothing but plains rolling up to the farther skyline. He sat down to wait, getting up every few minutes to take another look round. He certainly was excited.

At last the sky grew dark and a few stars lit up. Hare began to strut about so that the moon should see what a fine figure of a creature was waiting for her. He looked first down one side of the hill, then down the other. But she was still nowhere in sight.

Suddenly he saw her – but not coming up his hill. No. There was a black hill on the skyline, much farther to the East, and she was just peeping silver over the top of that.

'Ah!' cried Hare. 'I've been waiting on the wrong hill. I'll miss her if I don't hurry.'

He set off towards her at a run. How he ran. Down into the dark valley, and up the hill to the top. But what a surprise he got there! The moon had gone. Ahead of him, across another valley, was another skyline, another black hill – and that was the hill the moon was climbing.

'Wait for me! Wait!' Hare cried, and set off again down into the valley.

When he got to the top of that hill he groaned. And no wonder. Far ahead of him was another dark skyline, and another hill – and on top of that hill was the moon standing tiptoe, ready to fly off up the sky.

Without a pause he set off again. His paws were like wings. He ran on the tops of the grass, he ran so fast.

By the time he got to the top of this hill, he saw he was too late. The moon was well up into the sky above him.

'I've missed her!' he cried. 'I'm too late! Oh, what will she think of me!'

And he began leaping up towards her, calling:

'Moon! Moon! I'm here! I've come to marry you.'

But she sailed on up the black sky, round and bright, much too far away to hear. Hare jumped a somersault in pure vexation. Then he began to listen – he stretched up his ears. Perhaps she was saying terrible things about him – or perhaps, yes, perhaps flattering things. Perhaps she wanted to marry him much too much ever to think badly of him. After all, he was so handsome.

All that night he gazed up at the moon and listened. Every minute she seemed more and more beautiful. He dreamed how it would be, living in her palace. He would become a king, of course, if she were a queen.

All at once he noticed that she was beginning to come down the other side of the sky, towards a black hill in the West.

'This time I'll be waiting for her,' he cried, and set off.

But it was just the same. When he got to the top of the hill she was no longer there, but on the farther hill. And when he got to the top of that, she was on the next. And when he got to that, she had gone down behind the farthest hills.

Hare was furious with himself.

'It's my own fault,' he cried. 'It's because I'm so slow. I must be there on time, then I shan't have to run after her. To miss the chance of marrying the moon, and becoming a king, all out of pure slowness!'

That day he told the animals that he was courting the moon, but that the marriage day was not fixed yet. He strutted in front of them, and stroked his fur – after all, he was the creature who was going to marry the moon.

He was so busy being vain, he never noticed how the other creatures smiled as they turned away. Hare had fallen for their trick completely.

That night Hare was out early, but it was just the same. Again he found himself waiting on the wrong hill. The moon came over the black crest of a hill on the skyline far to the East of him. Hill by hill, he chased her into the East over four hills, but at last she was alone in the sky above him. Then, no matter how he leapt and called after her, she went sailing on up the sky. So he sat and listened and listened to hear what she was saying about him. He could hear nothing.

'Her voice is so soft,' Hare told himself.

He set off in good time for the hill in the West where she had gone down the night before, but again he seemed to have misjudged it. She came down on the hilly skyline that was farther again to the West of him, and again he was too late.

Oh, how he longed to marry the moon. Night after night he waited for her, but never once could he hit on the right hill.

Poor Hare! He didn't know that when the moon seemed to be rising from the nearest hill in the East or falling on to the nearest hill in the West, she was really rising and falling over the far, far edge of the world, beyond all hills. Such a trick the creatures had played on him, saying the moon wanted to marry him.

But he didn't give up.

Soon he began to change. With endlessly gazing at the moon he began to get the moonlight in his eyes, giving him a wild, startled look. And with racing from hill to hill he grew to be a wonderful runner. Especially up the hills – he just shot up them. And from leaping to reach her when he was too late, he came to be a great leaper. And from listening and listening, all through the night, for what the moon was saying high in the sky, he got his long, long ears.

HOW THE
ELEPHANT
BECAME

THE UNHAPPIEST OF all the creatures was Bombo. Bombo didn't know what to become. At one time he thought he might make a fairly good horse. At another time he thought that perhaps he was meant to be a kind of bull. But it was no good. Not only the horses, but all the other creatures too, gathered to laugh at him when he tried to be a horse. And when he tried to be a bull, the bulls just walked away shaking their heads.

'Be yourself,' they all said.

Bombo sighed. That's all he ever heard: 'Be yourself. Be yourself.' What was himself? That's what he wanted to know.

So most of the time he just stood, with sad eyes, letting the wind blow his ears this way and that, while the other creatures raced around him and above him, perfecting themselves.

'I'm just stupid,' he said to himself. 'Just stupid and slow and I shall never become anything.'

That was his main trouble, he felt sure. He was much too slow and clumsy – and so big! None of the other creatures were anywhere near so big. He searched hard to find another creature as big as he was, but there was not one. This made him feel all the more silly and in the way.

But this was not all. He had great ears that flapped and hung, and a long, long nose. His nose was useful. He could pick things up with it. But none of the other creatures had a nose anything like it. They all had small neat noses, and they laughed at his. In fact, with that, and his ears, and his long white sticking-out tusks, he was a sight.

As he stood, there was a sudden thunder of hooves. Bombo looked up in alarm.

'Aside, aside, aside!' roared a huge voice. 'We're going down to drink.'

Bombo managed to force his way backwards into a painful clump of thornbushes, just in time to let Buffalo charge past with all his family. Their long black bodies shone, their curved horns tossed, their tails screwed and curled, as they pounded down towards the water in a cloud of dust. The earth shook under them.

'There's no doubt,' said Bombo, 'who they are. If only I could be as sure of what I am as Buffalo is of what he is.'

Then he pulled himself together.

'To be myself,' he said aloud, 'I shall have to do something that no other creature does. Lion roars and pounces, and Buffalo charges up and down bellowing. Each of these creatures does something that no other creature does. So. What shall I do?'

He thought hard for a minute.

Then he lay down, rolled over on to his back, and waved his four great legs in the air. After that he stood on his head and lifted his hind legs straight up as if he were going to sunburn the soles of his feet. From this position, he lowered himself back on to his four feet, stood up and looked round. The others should soon get to know me by that, he thought.

Nobody was in sight, so he waited until a pack of wolves appeared on the horizon. Then he began again. On to his back, his legs in the air, then on to his head, and his hind legs straight up.

'Phew!' he grunted, as he lowered himself. 'I shall need some practice before I can keep this up for long.'

When he stood up and looked round him this second time, he got a shock. All the animals were round him in a ring, rolling on their sides with laughter.

'Do it again! Oh, do it again!' they were crying, as they rolled and laughed.

'Do it again. Oh, I shall die with laughter. Oh, my sides, my sides!'

Bombo stared at them in horror.

After a few minutes the laughter died down.

'Come on!' roared Lion. 'Do it again and make us laugh. You look so silly when you do it.'

But Bombo just stood. This was much worse than imitating some other animal. He had never made them laugh so much before.

He sat down and pretended to be inspecting one of his feet, as if he were alone. And, one by one, now that there was nothing to laugh at, the other animals walked away, still chuckling over what they had seen.

'Next show same time tomorrow!' shouted Fox, and they all burst out laughing again.

Bombo sat, playing with his foot, letting the tears trickle down his long nose.

Well, he'd had enough. He'd tried to be himself, and all the animals had laughed at him.

That night he waded out to a small island in the middle of the great river that ran through the forest. And there, from then on, Bombo lived alone, seen by nobody but the little birds and a few beetles.

One night, many years later, Parrot suddenly screamed and flew up into the air above the trees. All his feathers were singed. The forest was on fire.

Within a few minutes, the animals were running for their lives. Jaguar, Wolf, Stag, Cow, Bear, Sheep, Cockerel, Mouse, Giraffe — all were running side by side and jumping over each other to get away from the flames. Behind them, the fire came through the treetops like a terrific red wind.

'Oh dear! Oh dear! Our houses, our children!' cried the animals.

Lion and Buffalo were running along with the rest.

'The fire will go as far as the forest goes, and the forest goes on for ever,' they cried, and ran with the sparks falling into their hair. On and on they ran, hour after hour, and all they could hear was the thunder of the fire at their tails.

On into the middle of the next day, and still they were running.

At last they came to the wide, deep, swift river. They could go no further. Behind them the fire boomed as it leapt from tree to tree. Smoke lay so thickly over the forest and the river that the sun could not be seen. The animals floundered in the shallows at the river's edge, trampling the banks to mud, treading on each other, coughing and sneezing in the white ashes that were falling thicker than thick snow out of the cloud of smoke. Fox sat on Sheep and Sheep sat on Rhinoceros.

They all set up a terrible roaring, wailing, crying, howling, moaning sound. It seemed like the end of the animals. The fire came nearer, bending over them like a thundering roof, while the black river swirled and rumbled beside them.

Out on his island stood Bombo, admiring the fire which made a fine sight through the smoke with its high spikes of red flame. He knew he was quite

safe on his island. The fire couldn't cross that great stretch of water very easily.

At first he didn't see the animals crowding low by the edge of the water. The smoke and ash were too thick in the air. But soon he heard them. He recognized Lion's voice shouting:

'Keep ducking yourselves in the water. Keep your fur wet and the sparks will not burn you.'

And the voice of Sheep crying:

'If we duck ourselves we're swept away by the river.'

And the other creatures – Gnu, Ferret, Cobra, Partridge, crying:

'We must drown or burn. Good-bye, brothers and sisters!'

It certainly did seem like the end of the animals.

Without a pause, Bombo pushed his way into the water. The river was deep, the current heavy and fierce, but Bombo's legs were both long and strong. Burnt trees, that had fallen into the river higher up and were drifting down, banged against him, but he hardly felt them.

In a few minutes he was coming up into shallow water towards the animals. He was almost too late. The flames were forcing them, step by step, into the river, where the current was snatching them away.

Lion was sitting on Buffalo, Wolf was sitting on Lion, Wildcat on Wolf, Badger on Wildcat, Cockerel on Badger, Rat on Cockerel, Weasel on Rat, Lizard on Weasel, Tree-Creeper on Lizard, Harvest Mouse on Tree-Creeper, Beetle on Harvest Mouse, Wasp on Beetle, and on top of Wasp, Ant, gazing at the raging flames through his spectacles and covering his ears from their roar.

When the animals saw Bombo looming through the smoke, a great shout went up:

'It's Bombo! It's Bombo!'

All the animals took up the cry:

'Bombo! Bombo!'

Bombo kept coming closer. As he came, he sucked up water in his long silly nose and squirted it over his back, to protect himself from the heat and the sparks. Then, with the same long, silly nose he reached out and began to pick up the animals, one by one, and seat them on his back.

'Take us!' cried Mole.

'Take us!' cried Monkey.

He loaded his back with the creatures that had hooves and big feet; then he

told the little clinging things to cling on to the great folds of his ears. Soon he had every single creature aboard. Then he turned and began to wade back across the river, carrying all the animals of the forest towards safety.

Once they were safe on the island they danced for joy. Then they sat down to watch the fire. Suddenly Mouse gave a shout:

'Look! The wind is bringing sparks across the river. The sparks are blowing into the island trees. We shall burn here too.'

As he spoke, one of the trees on the edge of the island crackled into flame. The animals set up a great cry and began to run in all directions.

'Help! Help! Help! We shall burn here too!'

But Bombo was ready. He put those long silly tusks of his, that he had once been so ashamed of, under the roots of the burning tree and heaved it into the river. He threw every tree into the river till the island was bare. The sparks now fell on to the bare torn ground, where the animals trod them out easily. Bombo had saved them again.

Next morning the fire had died out at the river's edge. The animals on the island looked across at the smoking, blackened plain where the forest had been. Then they looked round for Bombo.

He was nowhere to be seen.

'Bombo!' they shouted. 'Bombo!' And listened to the echo.

But he had gone.

He is still very hard to find. Though he is huge and strong, he is very quiet.

But what did become of him in the end? Where is he now?

Ask any of the animals, and they will tell you:

'Though he is shy, he is the strongest, the cleverest, and the kindest of all the animals. He can carry anything and he can push anything down. He can pick you up in his nose and wave you in the air. We would make him our king if we could get him to wear a crown.'

By the same author

for children
Meet My Folks!
The Earth-Owl and Other Moon People
Nessie, the Mannerless Monster
The Coming of the Kings
Moon-Whales
Season Songs
Under the North Star
Ffangs the Vampire Bat and the Kiss of Truth
What is the Truth?
Tales of the Early World
The Iron Man
The Iron Woman
The Dreamfighter and Other Creation Tales
Collected Animal Poems Vols. 1-4
Shaggy and Spotty
The Mermaid's Purse